The Next Step After the Prayer of Jabez

THE Prayer OF
Abraham

I0149854

To God the Father, Who created all things.

To my Lord and Savior, Jesus Christ, Who paid the crowning price for my salvation.

To the Holy Spirit, Who lives in me and empowers me to carry out God's plan for my life.

To my wife, Karen, who has always prayed for me and believed in me when seemingly no one else did, not even me. Thanks for all your help with this book.

To our children, Tiffany, Heather and her husband Omar, David and his wife Leah, who are blessings to us.

And to our grandchildren, Emma, Penelope and Eleanor. I pray you fulfill God's plan for your lives.

Special thanks to my son David for his inspiration and motivation to write this book.

The Next Step After the Prayer of Jabez

THE Prayer OF Abraham

Understanding the Prayer of Faith

*A*dvantage™
INSPIRATIONAL

Michael Janiczek, DD

Library of Congress Catalog Number: 2010933010

Name:	Janiczek, Michael
Title:	The Prayer of Abraham
	Michael Janiczek
	Advantage Books, 2024
Identifiers:	ISBN Paperback: 978159751502
	ISBN eBook: 978159753315
Subjects:	Self Help – Personal Transformation
	Religion: Christian Life – Inspirational
	Religion: Christian Life – Spiritual Growth
	Religion: Christian Life – Self Help

Revised Edition - April 2024
24 25 26 27 28 29   10 9 8 7 6 5 4 3

Preface

Unlike the prayer of Jabez, which is a wonderful example of a general prayer from the Bible, the prayer of Abraham is an example of a specific prayer of faith for anyone who believes.

It is an example of a prayer for you to personalize for a crisis you are facing. In fact, the prayer of Abraham (a prayer of faith) has one condition that distinguishes it from other prayers, and I believe this makes it the most powerful prayer you and I can pray.

What is that condition? It must be a prayer for something you do not have, a situation everyone believes to be impossible. Something others look at and say there's no way for this to happen without God. You can argue all your prayers are like that and perhaps they are. However, through this study of Abraham, the father of our faith, I found out my prayer life caused me to come to a deeper understanding of what prayer is. And showing the difference between general prayers and the prayer of Abraham, which is the prayer of faith.

I studied the entire story of Abram and Sarai, which begins in Genesis 11:27 and continues through Genesis 17:5, when God changes their names to Abraham and Sarah. Parts of their story are also recounted in 1 Chronicles 1 and Nehemiah 9. Their story does not end in Genesis chapter 17. It goes on until their death and burial in Genesis 25:11.

Many parts of Abraham and Sarah's life are recounted throughout the Old Testament. Including mentions in the remainder of Genesis, Exodus, Leviticus, Numbers, Deuteronomy, Joshua, 1 Kings, 2 Kings. Also 1 Chronicles, 2 Chronicles, Nehemiah, Psalms, Isaiah, Jeremiah, Ezekiel, Micah, Matthew, Mark, Luke, John, Acts, Romans, 2 Corinthians, Galatians, Hebrews, James, and 1 Peter. In fact, Abram and Abraham are mentioned 262 times in throughout the Bible. (See a complete list of scripture references in the reference section of this book).

Since Abraham is the father of our faith, I recommend you study these chapters to get an understanding of his life and times. When I did this study, what I first found amazed me. As I began to dig deeper and gain more understanding about his story, I found some Biblical truths to apply to my life that have been extraordinary! It has energized and strengthened my faith and brought me closer to God than ever before.

1

My Accident

On October 4, 2010 I had a serious accident. I fell off the top of an eight-foot-high ladder in my garage and landed on a concrete floor. As I was falling, I had a thought not to land on my head, which could have been fatal, or on my hands or arms, which could have caused broken arms, wrists, or hands. I could turn my body, so I landed on my left side just above my hip.

When I landed, I had severe pain so much so I couldn't move. I began to scream for help and then began crying out that God would heal me.

My wife Karen and a neighbor soon arrived. Karen began to pray for me and tried to help me, except I was like a wounded animal, writhing in pain. I could move my arms and legs, but any movement of my body was impossible because of the pain on my left side.

They were trying to help me get up, only I would not let them touch or move me at first. I would scream in pain in one breath and ask God to heal me in the next. Karen called our son David, who was studying to EMT-paramedic, to come home immediately.

After a few minutes David arrived home and they lifted me up to my feet; and in great pain, I slowly walked into my house.

The pain in my side was "off the scale," it felt like I being hit by a car or beat with a baseball bat. I could not bend at the waist or become comfortable standing, so I was trying to sit down. I could not do that either, so I dove onto the couch and laid flat on my back. Unfortunately, even that was not comforting as the pain was non-stop and not getting better.

David and Karen laid hands on me and prayed I would be healed. After evaluating my body, David advised I might have internal injuries and needed to get to the hospital as soon as possible.

The pain felt internal to me, as if there was something broken or burst inside of me. I would not allow them to call for an ambulance, so they picked me up off the couch and got me in the car and off to the hospital.

I ended up in there for 3 days. I'd broken 2 ribs, broken vertebrae processes on four vertebrae (L1-L4) and a contusion on my spleen.

I did not want to be in the hospital for several reasons, 1) I believed God would heal me. 2) I did not have health insurance and 3) I just did not want to be at the hospital!

The Doctor's report was I was to be in the hospital for many days and probably in traction where I couldn't get out of bed for 4 to 6 weeks. By 12 weeks the bones would be healed, and I would possibly walk again. And by 5 months I may be back to normal, if all went well.

My wife, Karen, my son, David, and I prayed immediately and thanks to Twitter and Facebook, within minutes, family and friends all around the world were praying for me.

Karen called two key people. One was our Pastor and the other a prophet friend of ours from Ghana named Forson Swanzy. She told them what happened and they both said they would pray.

So there I was, in the hospital, in great pain with the doctors ordering blood tests, X-rays, MRI's and CAT scans. They took me for a CAT-scan rather quickly. While I was lying there on the table inside this tube I cried out to God, "Why am I here?" God immediately said to me, "Relax and everything will be fine. I will get all the glory from this and not to worry because all the bills would be taken care of."

So I laid there and God's peace came upon me and for the first time in hours of my accident I was at peace. Yes, still in pain, yet at peace.

This is how awesome God is. The same time I was getting my CAT scan and God was talking to me; Swanzy called my wife back and said "God told me to tell you to have peace in the situation. That God would be glorified by this accident and the hospital bills would be paid in full."

When I came back to my room from the MRI and CAT scan tests, Karen told me what our friend Swanzy said and I told her God told me the same thing.

That night the doctors told me they decided to transfer me to another hospital, which had a special trauma unit. Now in the natural I was thinking another bill to be paid, except in the spirit I knew God was in control.

At the hospital they gave me morphine for the pain. The drugs dulled my pain enough for me to tolerate it. The side effects knocked me out so I slept most of the time, only to wake up as the effects of the drugs wore off and I began to feel the pain again.

God's report is that one of the benefits of being a believer in Christ is that by Jesus' stripes, I am healed.

> *But he was wounded for our transgressions; he was bruised for our iniquities; the chastisement of our peace was upon him; and with his stripes we are healed (Isaiah: 53:5)*

> *Who his own self-bare our sins in his own body on the tree that we, being dead to sins, should live unto righteousness by whose stripes ye were healed. (1 Peter 2:24)*

I could not get out of bed without help, and once up I could not stand up straight or even walk very well. I was in much pain and all around me the doctors and nurses were telling me how bad things were. Despite all of that, I chose to believe God's Word, which said I was healed!

I was determined to get out of the hospital and get home soon. Even though the doctors said I would be bedridden, I refused to stay in bed. Within twelve hours of my accident I was out of bed. Granted, I needed help to get up and out. And I could not stand up straight; nevertheless, I would walk to the bathroom and then take a lap or two around the hospital ward before retuning to my bed.

It was not easy to do because the pain was so severe I could barely move. Nevertheless, I never stopped walking, confessing and acting like I was healed.

My nurses would come to the room looking for me and I would be walking in the hall. They told me I should stay in bed, but I told them I was going to be healed and have a quick recovery.

In fact, Karen and I kept telling everyone I would have a quick recovery and total healing. Despite what the doctors said and in the midst of the pain I was in. And even with the obvious limitations I had because of the condition of my body, I refused to do or say anything except **I was healed.**

Later, Karen told me she had so much faith God would heal me that when she came to the hospital on the next day she expected to find me completely healed. But instead I was still the same and the doctors were saying I might need surgery.

I wanted to go home the first night and fought with the doctors and nurses who kept insisting I needed to stay. They ended not doing surgery and sent me home after three days (the accident happened on Thursday afternoon and I went home Saturday morning).

My wife, Karen, and son, David, had to help me do everything. I could not get up or down from a chair without help. I could not lie in my own bed. On Saturday afternoon after I got home they had to buy me an automatic electric recliner for me to sleep in.

I just stayed in that chair all day and all night. Even though it was electronic I still needed help to get in or out of the chair. It took all Karen's strength to pull me up and out to walk or go to the bathroom.

I could not even wash or dress myself, as I could not bend at the waist other than to sit down, or stand up. That alone took several minutes to achieve with extreme pain with the help of Karen and David. I could do nothing by myself.

This went on for three weeks. During that time I had three distinct visits from God where He delivered healing to my body. I called them "God jolts" because it was like electricity jolting my body with healing power.

The first one came on Sunday morning the day after I came home from the hospital. Karen got me up, showered and dressed me. I decided to call my pastor to thank him for praying for me and to give a report to the church. He was teaching Sunday school, so I was leaving a message on his phone, when all of a sudden, God was all over me. I began to cry. I was trying to complete my phone message for the pastor all the while I was crying with God's power all over me. He later told me when he listened to the message he thought I was crying because of the pain I was in.

To the contrary, God was beginning to do a work on and in my body. I began to sing that song, "Wait and See, He's Not Finished with Me, Yet" by Brandon Heath. As I stood there in my kitchen, God's power began surging through my body. As I started walking around my house, I kept saying; "Yes God…more of that!" Because when God would send a jolt through my body, the pain would subside. I cannot tell you how good that felt!

Karen followed me through the house as I was getting my first "God jolt" God told her as she followed me, "Go and leave him alone, I am taking care of him. Go and get dressed."

I knew God was working on me and as the pain returned, I walked to the bedroom where Karen was getting dressed, and I said, "Let's go to church." She said, "When I awoke that morning God told me we were going to church. I told God, He better tell Mike we are going to church."

"When I saw you standing there with God all over you, I knew we were going to church, so I am getting ready."

It was not easy to get dressed or even to walk to the car and driving to church sitting in the passenger seat was a painful experience. Every bump and move worsened my pain, except when God tells you to do something you do it. I have learned to obey His voice.

When we arrived at church everyone was amazed to see me there. When my pastor saw me, it was as though he had seen a ghost. He could not believe I was there. He said, "What are you doing here? I got your voice message, and I could tell you were in a lot of pain. In fact, you stole my thunder. I was going to call you during the service and have the congregation pray for you." I told him God visited me that morning and I believed I was going to have a full and quick recovery.

I ended giving a testimony and preaching about God's healing power and how my body must line up with God's Word, which states "by Jesus' stripes, I _was_ healed!"

I walked back and forth in front of the church congregation that Sunday proclaiming I was healed and my body needed to line up with God's word which said I was healed.

Did I feel healed? No! Nevertheless, I kept saying, "I am healed...body fall into line with the Word of God."

During my recovery, which because of the pain medication was spent in a drug induced stupor, I tried to work and act like I was healed. I would not relent in my prayer and confessing of the scriptures. "By Jesus stripes I am healed." "Call those things which be not as though they were." I kept saying; "I am healed. My bones are healed. My spine, ribs and spleen are normal and I have no pain and I will have a quick recovery in Jesus Name."

I did this for two and a half more weeks in which time I received two more visitations from God.

On the third visitation, which was three weeks to the day of my accident, I was walking down my hallway to the bedroom and God's power was all over me. I started to cry and called to Karen. She came quickly and I started to hug her and cry, "God is all over me...He is all over me...God is all over me." And as I said this, still hugging my wife, suddenly I could stand up straight and all the pain stopped, just as I had been confessing!

You see, I could not stand up straight since the accident. I leaned way to the left. Suddenly I was standing straight up and the pain was completely gone. In fact, I did not take another pain pill and I have not had any pain since then. I was healed in that moment.

Everyone, including the doctors and nurses were amazed at my quick recovery.

It was my prayer and the prayer of my wife and son that confessed I would have a quick and complete recovery. That was our prayer of faith and our confessions matched our prayers.

As I now look back at that event, I realized I prayed "the prayer of Abraham" and I received exactly what I prayed for. That which was impossible, became possible, or I should say, it actually happened, because of my faith and the faith of those around me and the grace of God.

The interesting thing about that is the day after receiving my healing; we went to a Friday night church meeting where Apostle Dave Viljoen and his group AWC International were having an evening testimony service. Apostle Dave and his wife Deborah are from South Africa and God brought them to the Orlando area to start a ministry work here.

They work in the prophetic ministry. They knew of my accident and been praying for me for 3 weeks. They were amazed we were there that night and I could give my testimony of how God healed me in 3 weeks. After I finished testifying Apostle Dave turned to me and said, "I have a word for you." He said, "When you first met Norvel Hayes (whose Bible School Karen and I attended) he taught on a scripture verse and a principle. Go back to your roots and that word and so shall thy seed be."

I knew exactly what he was talking about. I knew because the first teaching I heard from Norvel Hayes, which changed our lives, was

Romans 4:17, which said, Abraham, like God, called those things which were not, as though they were.

The word from God that Apostle Dave had for me was to speak faith, to call those things which were not, as though they were. Looking back now, I realized I just did that very thing, which is what brought about the quick recovery and total healing I just received. Those words were my seed. The words (seed) I had sown (a quick recovery and complete healing) was exactly what I had received (reaped).

That is how this book came about. I began to dig deeper into Abraham's story where I found more of the same.

So then, there I was, 3 weeks after the accident, completely healed. The next Monday, the hospital and doctor bills started coming in. The total bill for the three days, tests and doctors was about $19,400.00.

I had already received the healing, however, the bill was still there. Karen and I continued to pray and believe what God said to me and to Swanzy, that not only would I be healed, the bill would be paid. I did not have that kind of money on hand, and in fact, because I had been out of work for three weeks, other bills were pilling up.

In addition to the hospital bills, I needed money to pay the normal living and business expenses. Those expenses, not counting the hospital bill were three times what was in my savings.

Miraculously, money started coming into my business from everywhere. I even received a notice from our bank they found a bank error in my favor in the amount of $2,000.00! That is something that happened to me before while playing the game Monopoly, only not in real life.

Before the month was over, all my business and personal expenses were paid up to date. I had more money in the bank than I started with. However, the hospital bill still loomed over my head, but the miraculous influx of cash to pay all the other bills was amazing. I knew God was working in our midst and we continued believing the hospital bill would be paid in full, as well.

Several months went by and it was now January of 2010. Nothing had changed regarding the hospital bill, so I decided to contact them to work out a payment plan. They had me fill out papers and said they would get back to me. That was a Monday morning.

The next day, Tuesday, a business associate and friend called me to his office. He is a jeweler and I do computer and convention work for him from time to time. He was going to pay me for some work I did recently. The amount he owed me was about $1,600.

When I went to see him, he said I had been a blessing to him for a long time, always there when he needed me, and he wanted to do something special for me. He then handed me a Rolex Sub-Mariner Wristwatch which is worth over $12,000.

He said he knew this watch was worth more than he owed me, only he wanted me to have it. I could not believe it. I went home to show Karen and she said, "You are very blessed." I told her, "Let's sell the watch and pay part of the hospital bill."

She looked at me and said, "You can't do that. What will you do when your friend asks you what happened to the watch he gave you? It was a gift, you can't sell it unless God tells you to sell it, and you need to keep it."

Like Abraham, I was trying to help God do something by taking matters He promised me into my own hands. I could not sell the watch my friend had given me, although it was tempting to do so considering my situation.

So we just continued believing the bill would be paid. Four days later, on Friday, I received a letter from the hospital. It said $19,200 of my bill had been paid and all I owed was $200!

God delivered on His promise. We immediately paid the $200 balance and the bill was paid in full!

Praise God Forevermore!

He is faithful to His word! Do not ever doubt God! He always comes through if we believe!

2

Who Do You Think You Are?

It seems it is human nature or desire to find out who we are and where we came from. Many of us are curious to see what kind of people we originated from and to see how far back we can go in our generations.

I have always wanted to know where I came from, unfortunately, I did not know a lot. Yes, I knew my grandparents and I only knew one great-grandmother, beyond that, I did not know anything else. That is because my ancestors migrated to America early in the 20th century.

In my wife Karen's family, her great-aunt Irene Stone-Geiger researched all the Stone family. She found ancestors dating as far back as the late 1200's in England. Thirty-five years ago when she did the research of her family, there weren't any computers for her to search with. But she was successful in finding the family lines throughout the centuries. We are now finding today with the help of Ancestry.com she was correct with all her information.

About a month after my accident Karen and I started to watch this television program that was on called, "Who do you think you are?" This was a program that took celebrities and helped them trace their roots. I found that week after week as I watched this I too had that hunger to find my roots. Where did I come from?

So I went on the computer to Ancestry.com to search for my roots. Ancestry.com uses records from many sources including U.S. and U.K. Census Collections, Voter Lists, Birth, Marriage and Death, Military, Immigration & Emigration, Newspaper & Periodicals, Directories & Member Lists, and much more.

Night after night I went to Ancestory.com and I could find information about long lost relatives from my past I never knew existed, even some relatives that went back hundreds of years.

Finding names, birthdays, marriage records and death certificates about relatives was enlightening and rewarding. It gave me a new sense of who I was and how my family immigrated to this country.

Even though this was a satisfying exercise, I still had a yearning to know more. Something else was tugging at my heart. I began to realize through this I was yearning to know my spiritual roots.

So I decided to go to the Bible and research my spiritual roots and since Abraham is called "the father of our faith" I decided Abraham was where I should start.

I suddenly realized God placed a true desire in me to find my spiritual ancestral roots. Researching these roots would require an in-depth study of the Bible. What I found was a wealth of information that has a great spiritual significance in my life.

If you think about it, if records existed, each of us should have roots back to Noah and from Noah, back to Adam and Eve. As I said before, I decided to fix my study on Abraham, because he was the one that Romans 4:17 was talking about. After all, the Bible says Abraham is the father of our faith.

Therefore it is of faith that it might be by grace. To the end, the promise might be sure to all the seed. Not to that only which is of the law, but to that also which is of the faith of Abraham; who is the father of us all. (Rom 4:16)

So, I began my adventure into my spiritual roots by studying all the scriptures related to Abraham. I found Abram (as he was named at birth) was mentioned 46 times in the Bible, and Abraham (as he was renamed by God) was mentioned 216 times. I started by reading those scriptures to find out everything I could about him. I advise you to do the same. If you turn to the reference section in the back of this book, you will find a list with all these scriptures for your convenience.

In short, Abraham was a man just like any other man. He had challenges in his family, with the government and religious leaders of his time and just like you and me he, sinned against God.

He had personal problems in his marriage, family difficulties, family disputes, an enemy trying to kill, steal and destroy his family, while trying to deal with a promise he received from God in a dream.

Most of us would probably crumble under the pressures Abraham faced; however, God saw one thing about Abraham that stood out, and that was he never doubted what God told him. He was a man of enormous faith. Faith in God He would do what He promised.

Regardless of the odds, what anyone else said, what it looked like to him or any other member of his family, Abraham refused to doubt the promises of God and Abraham's faith never wavered.

My study of Abraham revealed an interesting fact I believe all of us need to understand. God had to teach Abraham how to eventually use his faith to receive the promises he was given.

Why did God have to teach Abraham about how to use his faith? Please indulge me as I recount some Biblical details about Abraham's life. It may seem tedious; however, it will reveal some important points from which we can learn a great deal about God and faith.

Abraham is first mentioned in the scriptures in Genesis 11:27. Abram was the first son of Terah. To give you perspective on when this was, Abram was born about 1996 BC, which were 352 years after the flood of Noah and 246 years after the tower of Babel incident.

At the age of 74, God first spoke to Abram and told him he should move out of the city of Ur of the Chaldeans to go into the land he would later show him. A year later, God again spoke to Abram and called him from his own country, kindred and father's house. At that time a promise of blessing was given to him. That is, in his seed, all the nations of the earth would be blessed. (See Gen 12:1-2, Acts 7:4-5)

Therefore, when Abram was 75 years old, he obeyed the call of God and moved. This journey took several turns and lasted about a year until Abram and Lot ended in Canaan where they agreed to Part Company. Lot chose to go to Sodom and Abram remained in Canaan where the Lord renewed His promise to possess the land and of his numberless posterity. In fact it is here God tells Abram his seed would number "as the dust of the earth." (Gen 13:16)

Eight years later, Abram was grieved because he had no heir. Once again, God renewed His promise, but He also taught Abram how to correctly pray the prayer of faith. The key is found in Genesis chapter 15.

And he brought him forth abroad, and said, Look now toward heaven, and tell the stars, if thou be able to number them; and he said unto him, so shall thy seed be. (Genesis 15:5)

God is telling Abraham, <u>tell</u> the stars, vocalize it, use your faith, call those things which be not as though they were (Rom 4:17) tell them your seed will outnumber them.

In other words, God was saying, show me your faith Abram show me you believe me by saying it. Say your seed outnumbers the stars. Go outside, look up at the stars and tell them your seed outnumbers them.

It was Abraham's belief and obedience to this charge that caused God to count his faith for righteousness.

And he believed in the LORD; and he counted it to him for righteousness. (Genesis 12:6)

Think about that. This is about 2,000 years before Christ and the faith of Abraham was counted to him as righteousness (right standing with God).

A few years later, Sarai, Abram's wife, was longing for that seed. After all, ten years passed since they came unto the land of Canaan, and she still had not given birth. She came up with the idea to give her Egyptian servant, Hagar, to Abram as his wife. Hagar conceived and when Abram was 86 years old, Hagar bore him Ishmael.

More time passes and Abram is now 99 years old. God makes a covenant with Abram concerning the seed of Isaac, who was to be born about a year later. God gave him the sign of circumcision, changing both their names Abram which means father to Abraham which means "father of many nations" and Sarai, which meant contentious to Sarah which means princess.

When Abraham was 100 years old and his wife Sarah was 90, their promised son Isaac was born unto them. (Gen 17:17- 21, Gen 21:1-7, Rom 4:19)

I recount all this Biblical detail to make you see a few important points about Abraham that can help you in your walk of faith.

God spoke to Abraham early in his life and gave him a word about his seed. It took him some time to understand what God meant and along the way God coached him. Once he learned to use his faith by speaking out loud and calling things which be not as though they were, it wasn't long before God brought all those dreams and desires to pass.

3

Where Do Your Dreams and Desires Come From?

Are you satisfied with your life?

A better question is, are you fulfilling God's Plan for your life?

Chances are if your answer to either of these questions is no, you are not and never will be as happy or successful as you can be or as God planned for your life.

God has a plan for your life, a plan He had in mind before you were born. He gave you desires and talents to fulfill this plan and if you delight in Him and believe Him, those plans will come to pass. God himself will see to it they do.

What dream or desire has God given you?

4Delight thyself in the LORD and he shall give thee the desires of thine heart. 5Commit thy way unto the LORD; trust also in him; and he shall bring it to pass. (Psalm 37:4-5)

I believe Psalm 37:4 has a dual meaning which we do not entirely understand. You can look at it two ways.

1) God puts the desires in your heart.

2) He will give you the desires of your heart.

In either event, verse 5 (***Commit thy way unto the LORD; trust also in him; and he shall bring it to pass***) is the condition for verse 4 (***Delight thyself in the LORD and he shall give thee the desires of thine heart***) to become true.

When you trust in God with all your heart, soul and mind, when you have faith in Him, He can do anything you ask or think. God will see to it you get what you are praying for.

He will fulfill your wildest dreams, dreams which He has given you in the first place and if you have faith He will see to it you are a success.

> *May he give you the desire of your heart and make all your plans succeed. (Psalm 20:4 NIV)*

Do you know Gods plan for your life? If you don't or if you are not sure, why don't you seek the Lord? After all, the Bible says:

> *And I say unto you, Ask, and it shall be given you; seek, and ye shall find; knock, and it shall be opened unto you. (Luke 11:9)*

Ask God what His plans are for your life.

In addition, take a personal inventory of your natural skills and abilities. If you have unfulfilled dreams and talents, there is a good chance those dreams were given to you by God (as we have covered in previous scriptures). The talents you have are specifically designed for you to fulfill God's plan for your life.

Let me give an example.

Are there things you can do or understand others struggle with?

Perhaps you are gifted with compassion or musically talented or have an understanding in a particular area no one else has.

Beware of self-indulgence in this personal inventory, because delusion can make you think you have a talent you really don't have. That can set you on a course that is opposite of God's plan for your life. Don't let personal desire or greed hinder your vision.

If you don't understand this statement, just watch an episode of American Idol. You will see people without any musical talent, who have been deceived by others or themselves, into thinking they can sing, when they can't carry a tune in a bucket.

I believe this deception is caused by personal desire or greed to do something or just to become someone famous.

A good way to check you are possibly deceiving yourself or driven by self-indulgence is to not push or force your way into fulfilling your dream. Ask God to promote you in your position. DO NOT SELF-PROMOTE!

If the dream or desire you are praying about is God's plan for your life, He will promote you without your involvement or persuasion.

Remember what happened to Abraham and Sarah when they tried to intervene and help fulfill Gods plan for their lives. The human race has suffered the consequences of that intervention to this day.

Think about it, Ishmael was the beginning of the Arab nation and look at all the turmoil that is in the world because of the strife between Arabs and Jews.

All this started with Abraham and Sarah taking things into their own hands to try to achieve a dream God gave them.

This brings me to another key point about Abraham and Sarah that applies to us today. They both made mistakes and were sinners, just like you and me, still that did not disqualify them from achieving God's plan for their lives.

I believe the devil has paralyzed some by convincing them their sin disqualifies them from receiving anything from God, so they don't even try anymore. This paralysis systematically strips a believer of all belief, because it causes them to accept any situation they find themselves in and turns them into faithless believers, which is an oxymoron. It takes faith to believe in the first place, except this deception of the devil has convinced believers their faith does not work anymore.

God warns us about this when He asks in His word, "Whose report will you believe?"

God looked at Abraham and saw his faith, which caused God to overlook other areas of Abraham's life, including sin. What? Are you saying Abraham was a sinner? Yes, indeed.

He directly disobeyed God when God told him to separate himself from your kindred. Abraham separated himself, although he took Lot with him. I am sure he reasoned Lot was like a son to him, except he was not his son. He was his nephew; his decision to disobey God later caused great grief when Abraham fought Chedolaomer and other confederate princes who overtook the region where Lot lived and took him and his household captive.

Abraham had to go to war to free Lot. His army defeated the enemy and rescued Lot and many other prisoners. (Gen 14:1-24)

Another time Abraham came up with the idea Sarah should lie about their relationship, saying she was his sister, to deceive the king. This happened twice. (Gen 12: 13-20 and Gen 20:1-18)

Why is this important?

Abraham endured many situations and circumstances, both good and bad. Some were the result of disobedience, sin or even taking things in his own hands, however, none of those had any effect on the way God looked at him.

It is obvious Abraham never let circumstances around him change his faith. In fact, in the midst of all these situations, Abraham's faith was counted to him as righteousness. Do you understand what that means? God called Abraham righteous, before he was a Jew and long before Jesus came to the cross, because of his faith.

And he believed in the LORD; and he counted it to him for righteousness. (Gen 15:6)

The Biblical truth Abraham found favor with God because of his faith alone should cause us to change our faithless behaviors and believe God in every situation. Those who do this and learn to walk by faith and not by sight will see many glorious things.

Those who don't will wallow in their problems while an ever-increasing erosion of their faith occurs. I believe this is the situation the church finds itself in today. There are more people who would describe themselves as Christians who no longer attend church for one reason or another. These people have been deceived into believing fellowship with the saints is not important. The devil is like a roaring lion, seeking who he may destroy, and those that have been isolated from the pack are usually first to be devoured.

It is my observation most of these now isolated believers never had a firm foundation in the word to begin with and therefore now have become easy prey for the devil. These isolated believers accept the situations they find themselves in and they believe that because of their sins, God won't help them. That is a lie from the devil.

God's Word teaches us we are the righteousness of God in Christ Jesus. Your sin does not get in the way of God's view of you. If you will show God your faith, just like Abraham (who is the father of our faith), God will bless you and answer your prayers of faith and give you whatever you ask or seek.

Think of all the scriptures that promise believers anything they ask or think.

²¹Jesus answered and said unto them, Verily I say unto you, If ye have faith, and doubt not, ye shall not only do this which is done to the fig tree, but also if ye shall say unto this mountain, Be thou removed, and be thou cast into the sea; it shall be done. ²²And all things, whatsoever ye shall ask in prayer, believing, ye shall receive. (Mat 21:21-22)

Jesus said we should have faith and not doubt. I think we miss it here more than we know. We say we have faith, except our words and actions are full of doubt and therefore we do not receive.

Hitherto have ye asked nothing in my name; ask, and ye shall receive, that your joy may be full. (John 16:24)

There are many Christians who think of God as being mean and angry God, one who wants us to suffer and live in poverty. Jesus teaches us to ask in His name and we shall receive so our joy will be full. This sounds like a God who wants us to have all the things we ask for and to be happy.

If ye abide in me, and my words abide in you, ye shall ask what ye will, and it shall be done unto you. (John 15:7)

The qualification for believers to receive anything from God is to abide in Him. How do we do this? Get in His word. It is in His word (the Bible) you abide in Him.

In the beginning was the Word, and the Word was with God, and the Word was God. (John 1:1)

⁴⁶For had ye believed Moses, ye would have believed me; for he wrote of me. ⁴⁷But if ye believe not his writings, how shall ye believe my words? (John 5:46-47)

Jesus spoke these words. Foremost you must believe the Bible is the Word of God.

I have ministered to many people in churches around the country who say they are Christians, yet say they are not sure if the Bible is God's word. Many say they cannot understand it so they don't read it every day. This is another lie of the devil that keeps God's people from walking in victory.

The belief the Bible is God's word is the foundation of Christianity, yet we have churches full of people who do not believe this truth. Then they wonder why they don't receive anything from God, or they criticize those of us who do believe.

²⁰Now unto him that is able to do exceeding abundantly above all that we ask or think, according to the power that worketh in us, ²¹Unto him be glory in the church by Christ Jesus throughout all ages, world without end. Amen. (Eph 3:20-21)

God is able to do more than anything we can ask or think. I don't know about you, although I have a huge imagination and can think of some amazing things. We have a God that can and will exceed those dreams if we only believe.

What do you need?

What is your dream?

What are the unfulfilled desires of your heart?

Get into God's Word, abide in Him and start believing Him for those things and see what happens.

Michael Janiczek

4

What Was The Prayer of Abraham?

The prayer of Abraham was plain and simply a prayer of faith. It was a prayer that believed for something that did not exist. It was a prayer for something that was impossible without God's intervention.

Remember, Abraham was told he would be the father of many nations. This seemed impossible because Sarah was barren. Nevertheless, Abraham believed God and did not doubt.

God then taught Abraham to confess he had that which he was praying for.

¹After these things the word of the LORD came unto Abram in a vision, saying, Fear not, Abram; I am thy shield, and thy exceeding great reward. ²And Abram said, LORD God, what wilt thou give me, seeing I go childless, and the steward of my house is this Eliezer of Damascus? ³And Abram said, Behold, to me thou hast given no seed; and, lo, one born in my house is mine heir. ⁴And, behold, the word of the LORD came unto him, saying, This shall not be thine heir; but he that shall come forth out of thine own bowels shall be thine heir. ⁵And he brought him forth abroad, and said, look now toward heaven, and tell the stars, if thou be able to number them; and he said unto him, so shall thy seed be. ⁶And he believed in the LORD; and he counted it to him for righteousness. (Gen 15:1-6)

God told Abraham to go outside look up at the stars and tell them his seed would outnumber them.

This event is also recorded in Roman 4:17 where it says Abraham *"...calleth those things which be not as though they were."*

This is the key to understanding what a prayer of faith is. It was not through the law (which had already been given to Moses) but it was through the righteousness of faith (i.e. being in right standing with God because of his faith).

¹³For the promise, that he should be the heir of the world, was not to Abraham, or to his seed, through the law, but through the righteousness of faith. ¹⁴For if they which are of the law be heirs, faith is made void, and the promise made of none effect. ¹⁵Because the law worketh wrath; for where no law is, there is no transgression. ¹⁶Therefore it is of faith, that it might be by grace; to the end the promise might be sure to all the seed; not to that only which is of the law, but to that also which is of the faith of Abraham; who is the father of us all. (Romans 4:13-16)

This proves the prayer of faith is for Jews and Gentiles alike and Abraham is our spiritual genealogical father. His example of faith can be used by believers and we can expect the same results.

¹⁷(As it is written, I have made thee a father of many nations,) before him whom he believed, even God, who quickeneth the dead, and calleth those things which be not as though they were. ¹⁸Who against hope believed in hope, that he might become the father of many nations, according to that which was spoken, so shall thy seed be. (Romans 4:17-18)

Here in the book of Romans, The Holy Spirit is referring to the story of Abraham and how in Genesis 15:1-6 Abraham was taught by God to speak out and call his situation as God told him it would. Not to speak words reporting how it looked in the natural, but to speak faith words that spoke the situation as it would become.

What situations are you facing?

Remember I told you I was facing months of recovery from my accident. The doctors were reporting to me what they found in the natural, I chose to believe the scriptures and to rely on God's word. I was speaking words of faith just as Abraham had done. I was calling those things that be not as though they were.

Did I see immediate results? No! Over the course of 3 weeks I saw my faith words I spoke out loud come to being. I did not just think them; I did not whisper them in prayer. No I spoke them out loud all the time. I told everyone God was going to heal me quickly.

Start praying and believing God for the answer and speak out the situation as it will be when the answer comes, regardless of what your eyes tell you. Remember, we walk by faith and not by sight.

Michael Janiczek

5

Faith

Now faith is the substance of things hoped for and the evidence of things not seen. (Hebrews 11:1)

...God hath dealt to every man the measure of faith. (Romans 12:3)

Plutonium is a powerful substance, the most powerful substance found in the earth. Left alone it has no useful purpose. However, when it is enriched, it has amazing power. Power that can be harnessed for good, like in a nuclear reactor that can provide energy, or bad, like in an atomic bomb that can have a devastating destructive power. But it is not the most powerful substance on earth!

Faith is the most powerful substance in the universe. Think about it. Faith the size of a grain of mustard seed and can change any circumstance you face in life.

According to the dictionary, Faith is the belief in God or the absolute confidence or trust in God to do the things for which He has promised.

Hebrews 11:1 tells us faith is the substance of things hoped for and the evidence of things not seen.

This literally means if you believe God, He will do what you ask. Because the Bible says faith is the substance of things you are hoping for. In other words, your faith is used as the material needed to create what you are asking for.

The Bible teaches us faith is:

Given to all men in the same measure.

For I say, through the grace given unto me, to every man that is among you, not to think of himself more highly than he ought to think; but to think soberly, according as God hath dealt to every man the measure of faith. (Romans 12:3)

Faith in the size of a mustard seed can move a mountain.

And Jesus said unto them, Because of your unbelief, for verily I say unto you, If ye have faith as a grain of mustard seed, ye shall say unto this mountain, Remove hence to yonder place; and it shall remove; and nothing shall be impossible unto you. (Matthew 17:20)

Faith is one of the nine Gifts of the Spirit which God gives to a person in need for a specific event.

[7]But the manifestation of the Spirit is given to every man to profit withal. [8]For to one is given by the Spirit the word of wisdom; to another the word of knowledge by the same Spirit; [9]To another faith by the same Spirit; to another the gifts of healing by the same Spirit; [10]To another the working of miracles; to another prophecy; to another discerning of spirits; to another divers kinds of

tongues; to another the interpretation of tongues (1 Corinthians 12:7-10)

Faith is part of the fruit of the Spirit which is grown by the believer who abides in God and in His Word.

22But the fruit of the Spirit is love, joy, peace, longsuffering, gentleness, goodness, faith, 23meekness, temperance; against such there is no law. 24And they that are Christ's have crucified the flesh with the affections and lusts. 25If we live in the Spirit; let us also walk in the Spirit. (Galatians 5:22-25)

Faith can save you from eternal damnation.

For God so loved the world, that he gave his only begotten Son, that whosoever believeth in him should not perish, but have everlasting life. (John 3:16)

Faith can do anything you believe it can do!

And all things, whatsoever ye shall ask in prayer, believing, ye shall receive. (Matthew 21:22)

God used faith to frame the universe by the faith in his words...

Through faith we understand the worlds were framed by the word of God, so that things which are seen were not made of things which do appear. (Hebrews 11:3)

God spoke out and things happened.

And God said, Let there be light and there was light. (Genesis 1:3)

God taught Abraham the same thing; you must speak it out (Call those things that be not as though they were).

If you are a believer, you already have utilized faith in your life. You've decided to believe in God. To believe His Son's name is Jesus who came to earth and died on the cross for your sins, and on the third day the Holy Spirit raised Christ from the dead. Jesus then ascended into heaven where He sits at the right hand of the Father. He then sent His Holy Spirit, the same Spirit that raised Christ from the dead, to dwell in you.

After believing that, what is it you can't believe? Why is it some Christians struggle with personal problems of all sorts? If you ask them, they do not really know. If you suggest it is a lack of faith, most Christians become very defensive.

Perhaps that statement is wrong, because each of us is given the same measure of faith. Therefore, it would be more accurate to state they are not using or activating their faith.

It is like having to go on a 250-mile trip with your car, which is all gassed up and ready to go, except you don't have the keys. You are fully capable of driving your car 250 miles. And your car has the potential to take you on that trip, you have the fuel to take you there, only without the keys, you will never even leave the driveway.

What is the key that activates your faith to get you what you need? Your words! **Speaking it out is the key.**

It is what Abraham was missing all those years he silently believed, although once God told him to speak it out, it came to pass shortly thereafter.

You and I are related to Abraham. We have the same spiritual DNA. All of us have been given the same amount of faith. In addition to everything Abraham had, we have a true record of all he did and all the rewards and benefits he received because of his faith.

We have no excuse not to gain similar results if we decide to trust God and believe in Him, just as our father Abraham did. I am convinced God will bless us and honor our faith with the same results Abraham received.

Michael Janiczek

6

Our Daily Confession

I am the righteousness of God in Christ Jesus.

No weapon formed against me shall prosper.

I am stronger today than I was yesterday, and I will be stronger tomorrow than I am today, because Your Word say's, they that wait upon the Lord, He shall renew their strength.

I walk in divine health, because God's Word says by Jesus' stripes, I am healed. Therefore, I confess my body is healthy.

I break any generational curse that would try to oppress my body and cause sickness or disease in my body, in Jesus' name.

I am greatly blessed and highly favored.

I am full of the anointing of the Holy Spirit.

Your Word declares that whatsoever things I put my hands to shall prosper. Therefore, I proclaim I have successful relationships with my family and friends.

I walk in the fullness of God's plan for my life and my ministry fulfills your plan and is vibrant and successful.

My businesses are growing and successful.

My personal finances are growing and successful.

Karen and I met in 1973. We went to the same high school together, H.L. Richards High School in Oak Lawn, Illinois. We knew each other except never dated until a few months after graduation.

A few months later we started dating. We were engaged to be married for about 13 months and in 1977, at the age of 20, we were married.

Six months later we heard the call of God on our lives and we quit our jobs and enrolled in Bible College together. After graduating from New Life Bible College in Cleveland Tennessee, we went into private life, raising a family (we have 3 children) and working as lay ministers in whatever church we attended.

I got a job in Christian publishing, working for Strang Communications as an advertising account executive for Charisma Magazine and then as director of sales and marketing for Creation House Books from 1987 to 2001.

From 2001 until 2004 I worked for Dake Bible Publishers, New Leaf Press and Thomas Nelson Publishing.

Then in 2004 I started Advantage Books, which publishes Christian books in all categories.

It wasn't until 2007 we felt the desire to become ordained ministers. We contacted our Bible College and found we had the qualifications, so in April of 2007, Karen and I were ordained by Norvel Hayes and Christian Harfouche in a special ordination service.

For the first time in our married lives, we began praying together and doing daily devotions together and God has been speaking to us and directing us every day.

Our business and family lives have prospered greatly since we began to abide in the vine daily. God has expanded our ministries to include preaching and teaching. Karen and I operate in the Gifts of the Spirit. She operates in the prophetic ministry, and I receive words of wisdom, understanding and revelation knowledge and I am a seer.

His Word has become the centerpiece of our lives, and He has blessed us in every way possible.

We are no different than you. The only things we do are to read and believe the Bible every day.

We confess about ourselves what God says about us (in His Word) instead of what we see or feel. We use our faith every day. With that, we have a daily devotion time where we study the Bible. Sometimes we do two devotionals a day. And we pray together daily. We activate our faith daily in our prayer lives. We are confessing what we believe for out loud, calling those things that be not as though they were.

I don't expect you to finish this book and instantly you will be studying and praying an hour a day. Start out small. Go to the bookstore and get a devotional. Ask the Holy Spirit which one you should choose on the shelf. We use one titled **Sparkling Gems from the Greek** by Rick

Renner. It does not matter what devotional you use, just pick one and use it every day. Have your Bible there so you can read the scripture verse for that day. Talk about it with your spouse or meditate on it throughout the day.

When you start to pray; simply talk to God. Just start out with a minute or two a day. If you try to pray for a specific amount of time you will probably fail.

Start out by reading your devotional, one scripture verse out of the Bible, and pray for a few minutes. Repeat that each day and you'll see your time with God grow. In fact, when you begin to talk to Him, he will talk to you, and you will begin to want to spend more time with Him. But remember to start out small and grow.

We are excited to see what God has in store for us in the future. He has given us a glimpse of the future and we constantly believe Him for it to come to pass.

Since our priorities have changed and we have found time to spend with God each day, our daily confession and prayers have developed and are still developing.

I know God will do the same for you. We are blessed to be able to share and disciple others to join in this journey with us.

References

Abram 46 times in the Bible

Genesis 11:26 And Terah lived seventy years, and begat Abram, Nahor, and Haran.

Genesis 11:27 Now these are the generations of Terah: Terah begat Abram, Nahor, and Haran; and Haran begat Lot.

Genesis 11:29 And Abram and Nahor took them wives; the name of Abram's wife was Sarai; and the name of Nahor's wife, Milcah, the daughter of Haran, the father of Milcah, and the father of Iscah.

Genesis 11:31 And Terah took Abram his son, and Lot the son of Haran his son's son, and Sarai his daughter in law, his son Abram's wife; and they went forthwith them from Ur of the Chaldees, to go into the land of Canaan; and they came unto Haran, and dwelt there.

Genesis 12:1 Now the LORD said unto Abram, "Get thee out of thy country, and from thy kindred, and from thy father's house, unto a land that I will shew thee."

Genesis 12:4 So, Abram departed, as the LORD had spoken unto him; and Lot went with him; and Abram was seventy and five years old when he departed out of Haran.

Genesis 12:5 And Abram took Sarai his wife, and Lot his brother's son, and all their substance that they had gathered, and the souls that they had gotten in Haran; and they went forth to go into the land of Canaan; and into the land of Canaan they came.

Genesis 12:6 And Abram passed through the land unto the place of Sichem, unto the plain of Moreh. And the Canaanite was then in the land.

Genesis 12:7 And the LORD appeared unto Abram, and said, "Unto thy seed will I give this land." and there builded he an altar unto the LORD who appeared unto him.

Genesis 12:9 And Abram journeyed, going on still toward the south.

Genesis 12:10 And there was a famine in the land and Abram went down into Egypt to sojourn there; for the famine was grievous in the land.

Genesis 12:14 And it came to pass, that, when Abram was come into Egypt, the Egyptians beheld the woman that she was very fair.

Genesis 12:16 And he entreated Abram well for her sake; and he had sheep, and oxen, and he asses, and menservants, and maidservants, and she asses, and camels.

Genesis 12:18 And Pharaoh called Abram and said, "What is this that thou hast done unto me? Why didst thou not tell me that she was thy wife?"

Genesis 13:1 And Abram went up out of Egypt, he, and his wife, and all that he had, and Lot with him, into the south.

Genesis 13:2 And Abram was very rich in cattle, in silver, and in gold.

Genesis 13:4 Unto the place of the altar, which he had make there at the first; and there Abram called on the name of the LORD.

Genesis 13:5 And Lot also, which went with Abram, had flocks, and herds, and tents.

Genesis 13:8 And Abram said unto Lot, "Let there be no strife, I pray thee, between me and thee, and between my herdsmen and thy herdsmen; for we be brethren."

Genesis 13:12 Abram dwelled in the land of Canaan, and Lot dwelled in the cities of the plain, and pitched his tent toward Sodom.

Genesis 13:14 And the LORD said unto Abram, after that Lot was separated from him, "Lift up now thine eyes, and look from the place where thou art northward, and southward, and eastward, and westward."

Genesis 13:18 Then Abram removed his tent, and came and dwelt in the plain of Mamre, which is in Hebron, and built there an altar unto the LORD.

Genesis 14:13 And there came one that had escaped, and told Abram the Hebrew; for he dwelt in the plain of Mamre the Amorite, brother of Eshcol, and brother of Aner, and these were confederate with Abram.

Genesis 14:14 And when Abram heard that his brother was taken captive, he armed his trained servants, born in his own house, three hundred and eighteen, and pursued them unto Dan.

Genesis 14:19 And he blessed him, and said, "Blessed be Abram of the most high God, possessor of heaven and earth."

Genesis 14:21 And the king of Sodom said unto Abram, "Give me the persons, and take the goods to thyself."

Genesis 14:22 And Abram said to the king of Sodom, "I have lift up mine hand unto the LORD, the most high God, the possessor of heaven and earth."

Genesis 14:23 That I will not take from a thread even to a shoelatchet, and that I will not take any thing that is thine, lest thou shouldest say, I have made Abram rich.

Genesis 15:1 After these things the word of the LORD came unto Abram in a vision, saying, "Fear not, Abram; I am thy shield, and thy exceeding great reward."

Genesis 15:2 And Abram said, "LORD God, what wilt thou give me, seeing I go childless, and the steward of my house is this Eliezer of Damascus?"

Genesis 15:3 And Abram said, "Behold, to me thou hast given no seed; and, lo, one born in my house is mine heir."

Genesis 15:11 And when the fowls came down upon the carcases, Abram drove them away.

Genesis 15:12 And when the sun was going down, a deep sleep fell upon Abram; and, lo, an horror of great darkness fell upon him.

Genesis 15:13 And he said unto Abram, "Know of a surety that thy seed shall be a stranger in a land that is not theirs, and shall serve them; and they shall afflict them four hundred years."

Genesis 15:18 In the same day the LORD made a covenant with Abram, saying, "Unto thy seed have I given this land, from the river of Egypt unto the great river, the river Euphrates."

Genesis 16:2 And Sarai said unto Abram, "Behold now, the LORD hath restrained me from bearing. I pray thee, go in unto my maid; it may be that I may obtain children by her." And Abram hearkened to the voice of Sarai.

Genesis 16:3 And Sarai Abram's wife took Hagar her maid the Egyptian, after Abram had dwelt ten years in the land of Canaan, and gave her to her husband Abram to be his wife.

Genesis 16:5 And Sarai said unto Abram, "My wrong be upon thee. I have given my maid into thy bosom; and when she saw that she had conceived, I was despised in her eyes. The LORD, judge between me and thee."

Genesis 16:6 But Abram said unto Sarai, "Behold, thy maid is in thine hand; do to her as it pleaseth thee." And when Sarai dealt hardly with her, she fled from her face.

Genesis 16:15 And Hagar bare Abram a son, and Abram called his son's name, which Hagar bare, Ishmael.

Genesis 16:16 And Abram was fourscore and six years old, when Hagar bare Ishmael to Abram.

Genesis 17:1 And when Abram was ninety years old and nine, the LORD appeared to Abram, and said unto him, "I am the Almighty God; walk before me, and be thou perfect."

Genesis 17:3 And Abram fell on his face and God talked with him, saying…

Genesis 17:5 Neither shall thy name any more be called Abram, but thy name shall be Abraham; for a father of many nations have I made thee.

1 Chronicles 1:27 Abram; the same is Abraham.

Nehemiah 9:7 Thou art the LORD the God, who didst choose Abram, and broughtest him forth out of Ur of the Chaldees, and gavest him the name of Abraham.

Abraham 216 times in the Bible

<u>Genesis 17:5</u> Neither shall thy name any more be called Abram, but thy name shall be Abraham; for a father of many nations have I made thee.

<u>Genesis 17:9</u> And God said unto Abraham, "Thou shalt keep my covenant therefore, thou, and thy seed after thee in their generations."

<u>Genesis 17:15</u> And God said unto Abraham, "As for Sarai thy wife, thou shalt not call her name Sarai, but Sarah shall her name be."

<u>Genesis 17:17</u> Then Abraham fell upon his face, and laughed, and said in his heart, "Shall a child be born unto him that is an hundred years old? And shall Sarah, that is ninety years old, bear?"

<u>Genesis 17:18</u> And Abraham said unto God, "O that Ishmael might live before thee!"

<u>Genesis 17:22</u> And he left off talking with him, and God went up from Abraham.

<u>Genesis 17:23</u> And Abraham took Ishmael his son, and all that were born in his house, and all that were bought with his money, every male among the men of Abraham's house; and circumcised the flesh of their foreskin in the selfsame day, as God had said unto him.

<u>Genesis 17:24</u> And Abraham was ninety years old and nine, when he was circumcised in the flesh of his foreskin.

<u>Genesis 17:26</u> In the selfsame day was Abraham circumcised, and Ishmael his son.

Genesis 18:6 And Abraham hastened into the tent unto Sarah, and said, "Make ready quickly three measures of fine meal, knead it, and make cakes upon the hearth."

Genesis 18:7 And Abraham ran unto the herd and fetcht a calf tender and good, and gave it unto a young man; and he hasted to dress it.

Genesis 18:11 Now Abraham and Sarah were old and well stricken in age; and it ceased to be with Sarah after the manner of women.

Genesis 18:13 And the LORD said unto Abraham, "Wherefore did Sarah laugh, saying, Shall I of a surety bear a child, which am old?"

Genesis 18:16 And the men rose up from thence, and looked toward Sodom; and Abraham went with them to bring them on the way.

Genesis 18:17 And the LORD said, "Shall I hide from Abraham that thing which I do?"

Genesis 18:18 Seeing that Abraham shall surely become a great and mighty nation, and all the nations of the earth shall be blessed in him?

Genesis 18:19 For I know him, that he will command his children and his household after him, and they shall keep the way of the LORD, to do justice and judgment; that the LORD may bring upon Abraham that which he hath spoken of him.

Genesis 18:22 And the men turned their faces from thence, and went toward Sodom; but Abraham stood yet before the LORD.

Genesis 18:23 And Abraham drew near, and said, "Wilt thou also destroy the righteous with the wicked?"

Genesis 18:27 And Abraham answered and said, "Behold now, I have taken upon me to speak unto the LORD, which am but dust and ashes."

Genesis 18:33 And the LORD went his way, as soon as he had left communing with Abraham; and Abraham returned unto his place.

Genesis 19:27 And Abraham gat up early in the morning to the place where he stood before the LORD.

Genesis 19:29 And it came to pass, when God destroyed the cities of the plain, that God remembered Abraham, and sent Lot out of the midst of the overthrow, when he overthrew the cities in the which Lot dwelt.

Genesis 20:1 And Abraham journeyed from thence toward the south country, and dwelled between Kadesh and Shur, and sojourned in Gerar.

Genesis 20:2 And Abraham said of Sarah his wife, "She is my sister." And Abimelech king of Gerar sent, and took Sarah.

Genesis 20:9 Then Abimelech called Abraham, and said unto him, "What hast thou done unto us? And what have I offended thee that thou hast brought on me and on my kingdom a great sin? Thou hast done deeds unto me that ought not to be done."

Genesis 20:10 And Abimelech said unto Abraham, "What sawest thou, that thou hast done this thing?"

Genesis 20:11 And Abraham said, "Because I thought, surely the fear of God is not in this place; and they will slay me for my wife's sake."

Genesis 20:14 And Abimelech took sheep, and oxen, and menservants, and women servants, and gave them unto Abraham, and restored him Sarah his wife.

Genesis 20:17 So Abraham prayed unto God; and God healed Abimelech, and his wife, and his maidservants; and they bare children.

Genesis 21:2 For Sarah conceived, and bare Abraham a son in his old age, at the set time of which God had spoken to him.

Genesis 21:3 And Abraham called the name of his son that was born unto him, whom Sarah bare to him, Isaac.

Genesis 21:4 And Abraham circumcised his son Isaac being eight days old, as God had commanded him.

Genesis 21:5 And Abraham was an hundred years old, when his son Isaac was born unto him.

Genesis 21:7 And she said, "Who would have said unto Abraham, that Sarah should have given children suck? For I have born him a son in his old age."

Genesis 21:8 And the child grew, and was weaned; and Abraham made a great feast the same day that Isaac was weaned.

Genesis 21:9 And Sarah saw the son of Hagar the Egyptian, which she had born unto Abraham, mocking.

Genesis 21:10 Wherefore she said unto Abraham, "Cast out this bondwoman and her son; for the son of this bondwoman shall not be heir with my son, even with Isaac."

Genesis 21:12 And God said unto Abraham, "Let it not be grievous in thy sight because of the lad, and because of thy bondwoman; in all that Sarah hath said unto thee, hearken unto her voice; for in Isaac shall thy seed be called."

Genesis 21:14 And Abraham rose up early in the morning, and took bread, and a bottle of water, and gave it unto Hagar, putting it on her shoulder, and the child, and sent her away; and she departed, and wandered in the wilderness of Beersheba.

Genesis 21:22 And it came to pass at that time, that Abimelech and Phichol the chief captain of his host spoke unto Abraham, saying, "God is with thee in all that thou doest."

Genesis 21:24 And Abraham said, "I will swear."

Genesis 21:25 And Abraham reproved Abimelech because of a well of water, which Abimelech's servants had violently taken away.

Genesis 21:27 And Abraham took sheep and oxen, and gave them unto Abimelech; and both of them made a covenant.

Genesis 21:28 And Abraham set seven ewe lambs of the flock by themselves.

Genesis 21:29 And Abimelech said unto Abraham, "What mean these seven ewe lambs which thou hast set by themselves?"

Genesis 21:33 And Abraham planted a grove in Beersheba, and called there on the name of the LORD, the everlasting God.

Genesis 21:34 And Abraham sojourned in the Philistines' land many days.

Genesis 22:1 And it came to pass after these things, that God did tempt Abraham, and said unto him, "Abraham", and he said, "Behold, here I am."

Genesis 22:3 And Abraham rose up early in the morning, and saddled his ass, and took two of his young men with him, and Isaac his son, and clave the wood for the burnt offering, and rose up, and went unto the place of which God had told him.

Genesis 22:4 Then on the third day Abraham lifted up his eyes, and saw the place afar off.

Genesis 22:5 And Abraham said unto his young men, "Abide ye here with the ass; and I and the lad will go yonder and worship, and come again to you."

Genesis 22:6And Abraham took the wood of the burnt offering, and laid it upon Isaac his son; and he took the fire in his hand, and a knife; and they went both of them together.

Genesis 22:7 And Isaac spake unto Abraham his father, and said, "My father" and he said, "Here am I, my son." And he said, "Behold the fire and the wood: but where is the lamb for a burnt offering?"

Genesis 22:8 And Abraham said, "My son, God will provide himself a lamb for a burnt offering." So they went both of them together.

Genesis 22:9 And they came to the place which God had told him of; and Abraham built an altar there, and laid the wood in order, and bound Isaac his son, and laid him on the altar upon the wood.

Genesis 22:10 And Abraham stretched forth his hand, and took the knife to slay his son.

Genesis 22:11 And the angel of the LORD called unto him out of heaven, and said, "Abraham, Abraham", and he said, "Here am I."

Genesis 22:13 And Abraham lifted up his eyes, and looked, and behold behind him a ram caught in a thicket by his horns; and Abraham went and took the ram, and offered him up for a burnt offering in the stead of his son.

Genesis 22:14 And Abraham called the name of that place Jehovahjireh, as it is said to this day, in the mount of the LORD it shall be seen.

Genesis 22:15 And the angel of the LORD called unto Abraham out of heaven the second time.

Genesis 22:19 So Abraham returned unto his young men, and they rose up and went together to Beersheba; and Abraham dwelt at Beersheba.

Genesis 22:20 And it came to pass after these things, that it was told Abraham, saying, "Behold, Milcah, she hath also born children unto thy brother Nahor."

Genesis 23:2 And Sarah died in Kirjatharba; the same is Hebron in the land of Canaan; and Abraham came to mourn for Sarah, and to weep for her.

Genesis 23:3 And Abraham stood up from before his dead, and spake unto the sons of Heth, saying…

Genesis 23:5 And the children of Heth answered Abraham, saying unto him…

Genesis 23:7 And Abraham stood up, and bowed himself to the people of the land, even to the children of Heth.

Genesis 23:10 And Ephron dwelt among the children of Heth; and Ephron the Hittite answered Abraham in the audience of the children of Heth, even of all that went in at the gate of his city, saying…

Genesis 23:12 And Abraham bowed down himself before the people of the land.

Genesis 23:14 And Ephron answered Abraham, saying unto him…

Genesis 23:16 And Abraham hearkened unto Ephron; and Abraham weighed to Ephron the silver, which he had named in the audience of the sons of Heth, four hundred shekels of silver, current money with the merchant.

Genesis 23:18 Unto Abraham for a possession in the presence of the children of Heth, before all that went in at the gate of his city.

Genesis 23:19 And after this, Abraham buried Sarah his wife in the cave of the field of Machpelah before Mamre; the same is Hebron in the land of Canaan.

Genesis 23:20 And the field, and the cave that is therein, were made sure unto Abraham for a possession of a burying place by the sons of Heth.

Genesis 24:1 And Abraham was old and well stricken in age; and the LORD had blessed Abraham in all things.

Genesis 24:2 And Abraham said unto his eldest servant of his house that ruled over all that he had, "Put, I pray thee, thy hand under my thigh."

Genesis 24:6 And Abraham said unto him, "Beware thou that thou bring not my son thither again."

Genesis 24:9 And the servant put his hand under the thigh of Abraham his master, and sware to him concerning that matter.

Genesis 24:12 And he said "O LORD, God of my master Abraham, I pray thee, send me good speed this day, and shew kindness unto my master Abraham."

Genesis 24:27 And he said, "Blessed be the LORD God of my master Abraham, who hath not left destitute my master of his mercy and his truth. I being in the way, the LORD led me to the house of my master's brethren."

Genesis 24:42 And I came this day unto the well, and said, "O LORD God of my master Abraham, if now thou do prosper my way which I go."

Genesis 24:48 And I bowed down my head, and worshipped the LORD, and blessed the LORD God of my master Abraham, which had led me in the right way to take my master's brother's daughter unto his son.

Genesis 25:1 Then again Abraham took a wife, and her name was Keturah.

Genesis 25:5 And Abraham gave all that he had unto Isaac.

Genesis 25:6 But unto the sons of the concubines, which Abraham had, Abraham gave gifts, and sent them away from Isaac his son, while he yet lived, eastward, unto the east country.

Genesis 25:8 Then Abraham gave up the ghost, and died in a good old age, an old man, and full of years; and was gathered to his people.

Genesis 25:10 The field which Abraham purchased of the sons of Heth there was Abraham buried, and Sarah his wife.

Genesis 25:11 And it came to pass after the death of Abraham, that God blessed his son Isaac; and Isaac dwelt by the well Lahairoi.

Genesis 25:12 Now these are the generations of Ishmael, Abraham's son, whom Hagar the Egyptian, Sarah's handmaid, bare unto Abraham.

Genesis 25:19 And these are the generations of Isaac, Abraham's son, Abraham begat Isaac.

Genesis 26:1 And there was a famine in the land, beside the first famine that was in the days of Abraham. And Isaac went unto Abimelech king of the Philistines unto Gerar.

Genesis 26:3 Sojourn in this land, and I will be with thee, and will bless thee; for unto thee, and unto thy seed, I will give all these countries, and I will perform the oath which I sware unto Abraham thy father.

Genesis 26:5 Because that Abraham obeyed my voice, and kept my charge, my commandments, my statutes, and my law.

Genesis 26:15 For all the wells which his father's servants had digged in the days of Abraham his father, the Philistines had stopped them, and filled them with earth.

Genesis 26:18 And Isaac digged again the wells of water, which they had digged in the days of Abraham his father; for the Philistines had stopped them after the death of Abraham and he called their names after the names by which his father had called them.

Genesis 26:24 And the LORD appeared unto him the same night, and said, "I am the God of Abraham thy father. Fear not, for I am with thee, and will bless thee, and multiply thy seed for my servant Abraham's sake."

Genesis 28:4 And give thee the blessing of Abraham, to thee, and to thy seed with thee; that thou mayest inherit the land wherein thou art a stranger, which God gave unto Abraham.

Genesis 28:13 And, behold, the LORD stood above it, and said, "I am the LORD God of Abraham thy father, and the God of Isaac. The land whereon thou liest, to thee will I give it, and to thy seed."

Genesis 31:42 Except the God of my father, the God of Abraham, and the fear of Isaac, had been with me, surely thou hadst sent me away now empty. God hath seen mine affliction and the labour of my hands, and rebuked thee yesternight.

Genesis 31:53 The God of Abraham, and the God of Nahor, the God of their father, judge betwixt us. And Jacob sware by the fear of his father Isaac.

Genesis 32:9 And Jacob said, "O God of my father Abraham, and God of my father Isaac, the LORD which saidst unto me, Return unto thy country, and to thy kindred, and I will deal well with thee."

Genesis 35:12 And the land which I gave Abraham and Isaac, to thee I will give it, and to thy seed after thee will I give the land.

Genesis 35:27 And Jacob came unto Isaac his father unto Mamre, unto the city of Arbah, which is Hebron, where Abraham and Isaac sojourned.

Genesis 48:15 And he blessed Joseph and said, "God, before whom my fathers Abraham and Isaac did walk, the God which fed me all my life long unto this day."

Genesis 48:16 The Angel which redeemed me from all evil, bless the lads; and let my name be named on them, and the name of my fathers Abraham and Isaac; and let them grow into a multitude in the midst of the earth.

Genesis 49:30 In the cave that is in the field of Machpelah, which is before Mamre, in the land of Canaan, which Abraham bought with the field of Ephron the Hittite for a possession of a burying place.

Genesis 49:31 There they buried Abraham and Sarah his wife; there they buried Isaac and Rebekah his wife; and there I buried Leah.

Genesis 50:13 For his sons carried him into the land of Canaan, and buried him in the cave of the field of Machpelah, which Abraham bought with the field for a possession of a buryingplace of Ephron the Hittite, before Mamre.

Genesis 50:24 And Joseph said unto his brethren, "I die and God will surely visit you, and bring you out of this land unto the land which he sware to Abraham, to Isaac, and to Jacob."

Exodus 2:24 And God heard their groaning, and God remembered his covenant with Abraham, with Isaac, and with Jacob.

Exodus 3:6 Moreover he said, "I am the God of thy father, the God of Abraham, the God of Isaac, and the God of Jacob." And Moses hid his face; for he was afraid to look upon God.

Exodus 3:15 And God said moreover unto Moses, "Thus shalt thou say unto the children of Israel, the LORD God of your fathers, the God of Abraham, the God of Isaac, and the God of Jacob, hath sent me unto you. This is my name for ever, and this is my memorial unto all generations."

Exodus 3:16 Go, and gather the elders of Israel together, and say unto them, The LORD God of your fathers, the God of Abraham, of Isaac, and of Jacob, appeared unto me, saying, "I have surely visited you, and seen that which is done to you in Egypt."

Exodus 4:5 That they may believe that the LORD God of their fathers, the God of Abraham, the God of Isaac, and the God of Jacob, hath appeared unto thee.

Exodus 6:3 And I appeared unto Abraham, unto Isaac, and unto Jacob, by the name of God Almighty, but by my name JEHOVAH was I not known to them.

Exodus 6:8 And I will bring you in unto the land, concerning which I did swear to give it to Abraham, to Isaac, and to Jacob; and I will give it you for a heritage. I am the LORD.

Exodus 32:13 Remember Abraham, Isaac, and Israel, thy servants, to whom thou swarest by thine own self, and said unto them, "I will multiply your seed as the stars of heaven, and all this land that I have spoken of will I give unto your seed, and they shall inherit it for ever."

Exodus 33:1 And the LORD said unto Moses, "Depart, and go up hence, thou and the people which thou hast brought up out of the land of Egypt, unto the land which I sware unto Abraham, to Isaac, and to Jacob, saying, "Unto thy seed will I give it."

Leviticus 26:42 Then will I remember my covenant with Jacob, and also my covenant with Isaac, and also my covenant with Abraham will I remember; and I will remember the land.

Numbers 32:11 Surely none of the men that came up out of Egypt, from twenty years old and upward, shall see the land which I sware unto Abraham, unto Isaac, and unto Jacob; because they have not wholly followed me.

Deuteronomy 1:8 Behold, I have set the land before you. Go in and possess the land which the LORD sware unto your fathers, Abraham, Isaac, and Jacob, to give unto them and to their seed after them.

Deuteronomy 6:10 And it shall be, when the LORD thy God shall have brought thee into the land which he sware unto thy fathers, to Abraham, to Isaac, and to Jacob, to give thee great and goodly cities, which thou buildedst not.

Deuteronomy 9:5 Not for thy righteousness, or for the uprightness of thine heart, dost thou go to possess their land; but for the wickedness of these nations the LORD thy God doth drive them out from before thee, and that he may perform the word which the LORD sware unto thy fathers, Abraham, Isaac, and Jacob.

Deuteronomy 9:27 Remember thy servants, Abraham, Isaac, and Jacob; look not unto the stubbornness of this people, nor to their wickedness, nor to their sin.

Deuteronomy 29:13 That he may establish thee to day for a people unto himself, and that he may be unto thee a God, as he hath said unto thee, and as he hath sworn unto thy fathers, to Abraham, to Isaac, and to Jacob.

Deuteronomy 30:20 That thou mayest love the LORD thy God, and that thou mayest obey his voice, and that thou mayest cleave unto him; for he is thy life, and the length of thy days, that thou mayest dwell in the land which the LORD sware unto thy fathers, to Abraham, to Isaac, and to Jacob, to give them.

Deuteronomy 34:4 And the LORD said unto him, "This is the land which I sware unto Abraham, unto Isaac, and unto Jacob, saying, 'I will give it unto thy seed. I have caused thee to see it with thine eyes, but thou shalt not go over thither'."

<u>Joshua 24:2</u> And Joshua said unto all the people, "Thus saith the LORD God of Israel, 'Your fathers dwelt on the other side of the flood in old time, even Terah, the father of Abraham, and the father of Nachor; and they served other gods'."

<u>Joshua 24:3</u> And I took your father Abraham from the other side of the flood, and led him throughout all the land of Canaan, and multiplied his seed, and gave him Isaac.

<u>1 Kings 18:36</u> And it came to pass at the time of the offering of the evening sacrifice, that Elijah the prophet came near, and said, "LORD God of Abraham, Isaac, and of Israel, let it be known this day that thou art God in Israel, and that I am thy servant, and that I have done all these things at thy word."

<u>2 Kings 13:23</u> And the LORD was gracious unto them, and had compassion on them, and had respect unto them, because of his covenant with Abraham, Isaac, and Jacob, and would not destroy them, neither cast he them from his presence as yet.

<u>1 Chronicles 1:27</u> Abram; the same is Abraham.

<u>1 Chronicles 1:28</u> The sons of Abraham; Isaac, and Ishmael.

<u>1 Chronicles 1:34</u> And Abraham begat Isaac. The sons of Isaac; Esau and Israel.

<u>1 Chronicles 16:16</u> Even of the covenant which he made with Abraham, and of his oath unto Isaac.

1 Chronicles 29:18 O LORD God of Abraham, Isaac, and of Israel, our fathers, keep this for ever in the imagination of the thoughts of the heart of thy people, and prepare their heart unto thee.

2 Chronicles 20:7 Art not thou our God, who didst drive out the inhabitants of this land before thy people Israel, and gavest it to the seed of Abraham thy friend for ever?

2 Chronicles 30:6 So the posts went with the letters from the king and his princes throughout all Israel and Judah, and according to the commandment of the king, saying, "Ye children of Israel, turn again unto the LORD God of Abraham, Isaac, and Israel, and he will return to the remnant of you, that are escaped out of the hand of the kings of Assyria."

Nehemiah 9:7 Thou art the LORD the God, who didst choose Abram, and broughtest him forth out of Ur of the Chaldees, and gavest him the name of Abraham.

Psalm 47:9 The princes of the people are gathered together, even the people of the God of Abraham; for the shields of the earth belong unto God: he is greatly exalted.

Psalm 105:6 O ye seed of Abraham his servant, ye children of Jacob his chosen.

Psalm 105:9 Which covenant he made with Abraham, and his oath unto Isaac;

Psalm 105:42 For he remembered his holy promise, and Abraham his servant.

Isaiah 29:22 Therefore thus saith the LORD, who redeemed Abraham, concerning the house of Jacob, Jacob shall not now be ashamed, neither shall his face now wax pale.

Isaiah 41:8 But thou, Israel, art my servant, Jacob whom I have chosen, the seed of Abraham my friend.

Isaiah 51:2 Look unto Abraham your father and unto Sarah that bare you; for I called him alone, and blessed him, and increased him.

Isaiah 63:16 Doubtless thou art our father, though Abraham be ignorant of us, and Israel acknowledge us not; thou, O LORD, art our father, our redeemer; thy name is from everlasting.

Jeremiah 33:26 Then will I cast away the seed of Jacob and David my servant, so that I will not take any of his seed to be rulers over the seed of Abraham, Isaac, and Jacob; for I will cause their captivity to return, and have mercy on them.

Ezekiel 33:24 Son of man, they that inhabit those wastes of the land of Israel speak, saying, "Abraham was one, and he inherited the land; but we are many; the land is given us for inheritance."

Micah 7:20 Thou wilt perform the truth to Jacob, and the mercy to Abraham, which thou hast sworn unto our fathers from the days of old.

Matthew 1:1 The book of the generation of Jesus Christ, the son of David, the son of Abraham.

<u>Matthew 1:2</u> Abraham begat Isaac; and Isaac begat Jacob; and Jacob begat Judas and his brethren.

<u>Matthew 1:17</u> So all the generations from Abraham to David are fourteen generations; and from David until the carrying away into Babylon are fourteen generations; and from the carrying away into Babylon unto Christ are fourteen generations.

<u>Matthew 3:9</u> And think not to say within yourselves, we have Abraham to our father; for I say unto you, that God is able of these stones to raise up children unto Abraham.

<u>Matthew 8:11</u> And I say unto you, that many shall come from the east and west, and shall sit down with Abraham, and Isaac, and Jacob, in the kingdom of heaven.

<u>Matthew 22:32</u> I am the God of Abraham, and the God of Isaac, and the God of Jacob? God is not the God of the dead, but of the living.

<u>Mark 12:26</u> And as touching the dead, that they rise; have ye not read in the book of Moses, how in the bush God spake unto him, saying, "I am the God of Abraham, and the God of Isaac, and the God of Jacob."

<u>Luke 1:55</u> As he spake to our fathers, to Abraham, and to his seed forever.

<u>Luke 1:73</u> The oath which he sware to our father Abraham.

<u>Luke 3:8</u> Bring forth therefore fruits worthy of repentance, and begin not to say within yourselves, we have Abraham to our father. For I say unto you, that God is able of these stones to raise up children unto Abraham.

Luke 3:34 Which was the son of Jacob, which was the son of Isaac, which was the son of Abraham, which was the son of Thara, which was the son of Nachor.

Luke 13:16 And ought not this woman, being a daughter of Abraham, whom Satan hath bound, lo, these eighteen years, be loosed from this bond on the sabbath day?

Luke 13:28 There shall be weeping and gnashing of teeth, when ye shall see Abraham, and Isaac, and Jacob, and all the prophets, in the kingdom of God, and you yourselves thrust out.

Luke 16:23 And in hell he lift up his eyes, being in torments, and seeth Abraham afar off, and Lazarus in his bosom.

Luke 16:24 And he cried and said, "Father Abraham, have mercy on me, and send Lazarus, that he may dip the tip of his finger in water, and cool my tongue; for I am tormented in this flame."

Luke 16:25 But Abraham said, "Son, remember that thou in thy lifetime receivedst thy good things, and likewise Lazarus evil things; but now he is comforted, and thou art tormented."

Luke 16:29 Abraham saith unto him, "They have Moses and the prophets; let them hear them."

Luke 16:30 And he said, "Nay, father Abraham; but if one went unto them from the dead, they will repent."

Luke 19:9 And Jesus said unto him, "This day is salvation come to this house, forsomuch as he also is a son of Abraham."

Luke 20:37 Now that the dead are raised, even Moses shewed at the bush, when he calleth the Lord the God of Abraham, and the God of Isaac, and the God of Jacob.

John 8:39 They answered and said unto him, "Abraham is our father." Jesus saith unto them, "If ye were Abraham's children, ye would do the works of Abraham."

John 8:40 But now ye seek to kill me, a man that hath told you the truth, which I have heard of God; this did not Abraham.

John 8:52 Then said the Jews unto him, "Now we know that thou hast a devil. Abraham is dead, and the prophets; and thou sayest, 'If a man keeps my saying, he shall never taste of death'."

John 8:53 Art thou greater than our father Abraham, which is dead? And the prophets are dead, whom makest thou thyself?

John 8:56 Your father Abraham rejoiced to see my day; and he saw it, and was glad

John 8:57 Then said the Jews unto him, "Thou art not yet fifty years old, and hast thou seen Abraham?"

John 8:58 Jesus said unto them, Verily, verily, I say unto you, Before Abraham was, I am.

Acts 3:13 The God of Abraham, and of Isaac, and of Jacob, the God of our fathers, hath glorified his Son Jesus; whom ye delivered up, and denied him in the presence of Pilate, when he was determined to let him go.

<u>Acts 3:25</u> Ye are the children of the prophets, and of the covenant which God made with our fathers, saying unto Abraham, "And in thy seed shall all the kindreds of the earth be blessed."

<u>Acts 7:2</u> And he said, Men, brethren, and fathers, hearken; The God of glory appeared unto our father Abraham, when he was in Mesopotamia, before he dwelt in Charran,

<u>Acts 7:8</u> And he gave him the covenant of circumcision; and so Abraham begat Isaac, and circumcised him the eighth day; and Isaac begat Jacob; and Jacob begat the twelve patriarchs.

<u>Acts 7:16</u> And were carried over into Sychem, and laid in the sepulchre that Abraham bought for a sum of money of the sons of Emmor the father of Sychem.

<u>Acts 7:17</u> But when the time of the promise drew nigh, which God had sworn to Abraham, the people grew and multiplied in Egypt.

<u>Acts 7:32</u> Saying, "I am the God of thy fathers, the God of Abraham, and the God of Isaac, and the God of Jacob." Then Moses trembled, and durst not behold.

<u>Acts 13:26</u> Men and brethren, children of the stock of Abraham, and whosoever among you feareth God, to you is the word of this salvation sent.

<u>Romans 4:1</u> What shall we say then that Abraham our father, as pertaining to the flesh, hath found?

Romans 4:2 For if Abraham were justified by works, he hath whereof to glory; but not before God.

Romans 4:3 For what saith the scripture? Abraham believed God, and it was counted unto him for righteousness.

Romans 4:9 Cometh this blessedness then upon the circumcision only, or upon the uncircumcision also? For we say that faith was reckoned to Abraham for righteousness.

Romans 4:12 And the father of circumcision to them who are not of the circumcision only, but who also walk in the steps of that faith of our father Abraham, which he had being yet uncircumcised.

Romans 4:13 For the promise, that he should be the heir of the world, was not to Abraham, or to his seed, through the law, but through the righteousness of faith.

Romans 4:16 Therefore it is of faith, that it might be by grace; to the end the promise might be sure to all the seed; not to that only which is of the law, but to that also which is of the faith of Abraham; who is the father of us all.

Romans 9:7 Neither because they are the seed of Abraham are they all children; but, in Isaac shall thy seed be called.

Romans 11:1 I say then, Hath God cast away his people? God forbid. For I also am an Israelite, of the seed of Abraham, of the tribe of Benjamin.

<u>2 Corinthians 11:22</u> Are they Hebrews? So am I. Are they Israelites? So am I. Are they the seed of Abraham? So am I.

<u>Galatians 3:6</u> Even as Abraham believed God, and it was accounted to him for righteousness.

<u>Galatians 3:7</u> Know ye therefore that they which are of faith, the same are the children of Abraham.

<u>Galatians 3:8</u> And the scripture, foreseeing that God would justify the heathen through faith, preached before the gospel unto Abraham, saying, "In thee shall all nations be blessed."

<u>Galatians 3:9</u> So then they which be of faith are blessed with faithful Abraham.

<u>Galatians 3:14</u> That the blessing of Abraham might come on the Gentiles through Jesus Christ; that we might receive the promise of the Spirit through faith.

<u>Galatians 3:16</u> Now to Abraham and his seed were the promises made. He saith not, "And to seeds, as of many; but as of one, and to thy seed, which is Christ."

<u>Galatians 3:18</u> For if the inheritance be of the law, it is no more of promise; but God gave it to Abraham by promise.

<u>Galatians 4:22</u> For it is written, that Abraham had two sons, the one by a bondmaid, the other by a freewoman.

Hebrews 2:16 For verily he took not on him the nature of angels; but he took on him the seed of Abraham.

Hebrews 6:13 For when God made promise to Abraham, because he could swear by no greater, he sware by himself.

Hebrews 7:1 For this Melchisedec, king of Salem, priest of the most high God, who met Abraham returning from the slaughter of the kings, and blessed him.

Hebrews 7:2 To whom also Abraham gave a tenth part of all; first being by interpretation King of righteousness, and after that also King of Salem, which is, King of peace.

Hebrews 7:4 Now consider how great this man was, unto whom even the patriarch Abraham gave the tenth of the spoils.

Hebrews 7:5 And verily they that are of the sons of Levi, who receive the office of the priesthood, have a commandment to take tithes of the people according to the law, that is, of their brethren, though they come out of the loins of Abraham.

Hebrews 7:6 But he whose descent is not counted from them received tithes of Abraham, and blessed him that had the promises.

Hebrews 7:9 And as I may so say, Levi also, who receiveth tithes, payed tithes in Abraham.

Hebrews 11:8 By faith Abraham, when he was called to go out into a place which he should after receive for an inheritance, obeyed; and he went out, not knowing whither he went.

Hebrews 11:17 By faith Abraham, when he was tried, offered up Isaac; and he that had received the promises offered up his only begotten son.

James 2:21 Was not Abraham our father justified by works, when he had offered Isaac his son upon the altar?

James 2:23 And the scripture was fulfilled which saith, Abraham believed God, and it was imputed unto him for righteousness; and he was called the Friend of God.

1 Peter 3:6 Even as Sara obeyed Abraham, calling him lord; whose daughters ye are, as long as ye do well, and are not afraid with any amazement.

Michael Janiczek is available for speaking engagements and personal appearances. For more information contact:

Michael Janiczek
C/O Advantage Books
info@advbooks.com

Other books available from Michael and Karen Janiczek

Listen Up! How To Hear The Voice of God
ISBN: 978-1-59755-223-2

eWitness: Share your faith with daily inspirational Facebook posts
ISBN: 978-1-59755-272-1

To purchase additional copies of this book or other books published by Advantage Books, visit our online bookstore at advbookstore.com

*A*dvantage
BOOKS

Orlando, Florida, USA
"we bring dreams to life"™
www.advbookstore.com

www.ingramcontent.com/pod-product-compliance
Lightning Source LLC
LaVergne TN
LVHW011411080426
835511LV00005B/485